BEADS OF WORDS

Human emotions felt by all, focused by none.

Shruti Soni

ISBN 978-93-5458-554-8
© Shruti Soni 2021
Published in India 2021 by Pencil

A brand of
One Point Six Technologies Pvt. Ltd.
123, Building J2, Shram Seva Premises,
Wadala Truck Terminal, Wadala (E)
Mumbai 400037, Maharashtra, INDIA
E connect@thepencilapp.com
W www.thepencilapp.com

DISCLAIMER: *The opinions expressed in this book are those of the authors and do not purport to reflect the views of the Publisher.*

Author biography

BEADS OF WORDS' is a poetry genre book written by Shruti Soni , an eighteen year old writer. Her journey started when she was in class 7th. At start she use to write small poetries and compose song out of leisure and free time , but as the time passed she inculcated a sheer interest and started to pour her thoughts in form of rhymes and poetries.

She is an enthusiast and a sporty hodophile build up with happy soul and unlocked mind .

Her poems are generally based on Human emotions felt by all ,focused by none. By pouring her thoughts on paper she take it as an opportunity to give voice to the issues and emotions of people.

Initially her poems were published in school magazines and later in various international anthologies, giving wings to her passion.

She has a positive outlook towards life and tries to change the negative perspective of people through her writing and passion.

A believer of hard work she creates her own luck and encourages others to stay enthusiastic and determined in life.

This is her Debut Book

CONTENTS

Preface

Initially i never confronted with my ability of beautifying words through emotions.

At first, i use to write poems for small school acts or compose songs for school projects, but later on as i went on in life, i realised how soothing it is to pour our emotions on a piece of paper and create a beautiful poetic piece of work.

I usually write when the nature allows me, by provoking my thought process and giving wings to my emotions. Steadily i realised that not everyone is expressive and can bead their thoughts in a string so i started writing my poetic piece that were based on human emotions, eventually felt by all but expressed by few.

Writing is my strength and my way of enjoying life with a positive outlook. Things surrounding us usually have a great effect on our life and mental trauma. My poems by reflecting such emotions makes the reader feel soothing and connected and help him to stay positive even at times of hardships and despair.

Starting with publishing my poems in school magazines and various anthologies since i was in class 11th , i decided to not to chain my passion and fly high.

In times of COVID where there was mental and physical agony all over, my poems were my way of staying connected to my optimistic attitude and that is when i decided to utilise this time in a productive way.

The book is a composition of my poetic expression and collection of my fervour as a writer filled with hardwork and belives.

Acknowledgements

At first i would dedicate all my work to Lord Ganesha who filled me with such qualities and enthusiastic attitude that helped me to achieve my goals today .

Words fail to meet its height, when i express my heartfelt gratitude towards my parents who were my constant supporter and mentor throughout my journey.

I would also like to thank my teachers and mentors who always supported me and made me believe in my own self.

I would to like express my gratefulness towards my family mates for always appreciating my work and success.

I m also thankful to all my friends who insisted me to write more and more and always encouraged me to fly high.

I would also like to thank the Pencil publishing team for giving me an opportunity to publish my Debut book and helping me in my journey.

Introduction

BEADS OF WORDS' is a bewitching collection of emotions and motivational poems, that revolves around pouring human sentiments in words that are felt by all but focused by none. Times of hardships, sorrow, despair, strength and stimulation are the base of these poetries. The poetic pieces are of different nature, some aimed at igniting a ray of hope whereas some are focused on staying consistent at times of pessimism.

Optimistic and positive outlook towards life is the elixir of the book.

Life has a long way to go ...

Life has a long way to go

Hurdles passing by
Sometimes making me cry
Sometimes showering the happiness from the sky.

Carrying along untold happenings
Continues to make one's way.

I musing about my cup of coffee
Perplexed about what to do
Cheesed off of all the tantrums
Plotting up for a lofty layoff.

There betwixt the solitary nature
Debating with oneself
Finally getting through the tantrums
Provocating life with an unhackneyed ethos.

Clearing all the bamboozlements
Yet a long trail to be covered.

Passing all the hurdles by a weapon of jollity
A new soul got up
Not confusing

But conjecturing.

\- Shruti Soni

The Wet Soul...!

The sun sets
Moon escaped
Sky drizzling with clouds
and suddenly the echo was heard of the rain on the roof
For the soul broken and damaged
Lifts up her head
The drops run through her lips
Like a garland in a thread.
Dissolving her tears
They washed away all her perplexed thoughts
The soul was immortal
But the shell was not;
and suddenly breaking the chain of her pain
Her eyes rolled up , head lifted , hands moved , fingers entangled
For there was another soul
wet and moist
A bit late
But the soul got her mate
For this was her fate...!

-Shruti Soni

Another Shoot of Life...!

From dusk to dawn
I was all at sea
about my another shoot
Going to be ready soon.
My excitement was at my door.
Knocking down ready to take me to the shore.
For that unhackneyed and mysterious building
My eyes trying to behold its charm
Conceptualizing the succeeding window of opportunities
They started imagining
For the books going to be my mate
touching to core of my soul they will cover it
with a sheet of savoir faire.
The huge empty walls going to be the pages of my good
books
for they will enlight me with life.
For the pen to be my lover
decoding the beauty of moon teaching me to climb
another stair.
Trying me to taste failure
for the Sun too sets
After its triumph.
Molding the hot iron in a shape
to be perfect for
the third shot

My eyes trying to catch and hold
But the excitement in it
The mirror speaking to me
For its the time
to be ready
about my another chapter
going to start soon
My excitement was at my door
Knocking down
ready to take me to the shore.

-Shruti Soni

A Question yet Unanswered!

Her question was still unanswered.
Shattered defeated and overpowered she
The moon along with the stars witnessed it
Empty roads being perceiver
Yet helpless
Imprinting the fear in her heart
She find it hard to walk
Terrific eyes along with unspoken scars
and soul in a state of delicacy
But they don't had a spark of decency.
Romping around her
Unstoppable.
Clouds shattered , sun escaped
Yet betwixt the solitary nature
Debating with oneself
Figuring out her fault
Her question was still unanswered
Worn out and stunned
Was it really to be done ?

- Shruti Soni

Be Together!

Speechless night
Permeated with wishes allover
Those gleam of stars and Median moon
So close still too far.

Sod surrounding me
Making me feel cosy and secure
Enduring those sights
Flowers being my side.

My voice is to you mumbling my day
You hear it so patiently and have nothing to say.
Slowly the drops twinkling down
Touching my lips
Eyes capturing those mark
Encircling me with residue
Not humans but the near ones.

Not isolated but together
Close to nature
Near to every creature.
Nature has its own erection with all its
feel
Ushering us to be together
Needless

Isolation is a pill
That definately will kill.

- Shruti Soni

Being in Despair!

In that Rainy night
My Encephalon
Glooming with voice
Drops twinkling down my window pane
Palavering to me
Adoring my beauty
By reflecting the serenity
Blur but perfect picture
Of the love and care
Required by my self
Clear and fair
To vanish the thought of despair.

- Shruti Soni

Males too have heart!

Satirical words mostly
take us back to the traumas of females
Let's get a bit offtrack this time
Males too have heart ..!!!!

Wondering his mouldings
reposed near the sea
He drifted into reveries , abstracted , distrait
for the hassle in his life
faced by him
Focused by none

He snowed under sacrificies
and his mishappenings veiled under his smirk
carrying along unfathomable responsibilities
holding back his emotions bury
Coming up tough as old boots...

Their heart bounteous
Ungrudgingly managing all their plights and hiccups
with their smirk , constant and adore
for its the light a candle needs.

Lost in a noisy crowd
Hard pressed with duties

carrying together multitude buckets
filled with untold patches of time

For he is too a Son , a Brother , a Husband and a Father
though belonging to the same category
he flies differently..

For all Macho's are not Rapists
For all Masculines don't hit
For all Men don't scorn
For some Males too have heart.

This time let's get a bit offtrack
this time let's bequeath a note to him
with a voyage saying
"Males too have heart..!!!"

Shruti Soni

Homeage to unsung victims!

Down the town
Observing the happenings
Again the same news fled
One more girl , one more rape , one more life came to an
end!
What else to say!
What else to prove !
Is there any difference left between hell and this place ?
'Respect her , both are equal....' what all not to say
Just sayings , never followed.
One more girl ,one more life , again thè victory of the
crimes.

No strict punishment , no strict rules
Imagine your love ones in that queue.

Their souls graving for justice
But the cases just piling
One by one , again and again
No strict punishment , no strict action
Just a penalty of imprisonment
Is this the constitution
Having only prisons ?

Again the same news fled

One more girl , one more rape , one more life came to an end!
Imprinting the fear in the hearts of women
What else to say!
What else to do !

You talk about growth , here she find it hard to walk just because we are sloth.

Now you decide..what you want.

A place to be lived
Or a place to be killed!!
A country of divine
Or a country of vile !!

- Shruti Soni

My Angst Soul!

Down the lane
Betwixt thoughts
My soul tumult
Confronting the past
Vexed and a bit dread
Endeavouring to quell
Yet it dwell.

- Shruti Soni

Another Espouse!

A sleepless night
Teared and tortured
Like the twinkling starts
He was a pure serenity
Mollycoddling me
His every word
Full of love
Pure and admire
In the interim
I got another espouse
To fall a little more for him.

- Shruti Soni

Wings and cages!

She got wings
But was caged
Valorous and plucky
Running to conquer different phase.

-Shruti Soni

My forgotten book!

Beneath that limitless sky
I was sitting spare
Twinning with my thoughts
Glued in midst of the broken clouds
Musing about my forgotten books.

Wandering back in time
Today let's turn the pages
Admire the beauty it holds
Intentions so pure
In front of whose even gold has no allure.

Suprised by the clock
In a blink of eye
Fallacy was the new reason
New thought
And another season
Of tearing those pages
And forgetting those books....

- Ever tried to confront the one ?
- Ever introspected beneath the clouds wandering about the fallacies adoring that beauty of pages ?
- Ever wished to reverse your activities just to bring back your forgotten books ?

BEADS OF WORDS

- Shruti Soni

If Candies weren't that sour!!

Only if death wasn't a sweet lie
If gathering roses wasn't that hard
If the bars weren't that sorest
then the Candies weren't that sour.

Life would be watching grass grow
and everything would have been at the stroke of a pen
with the saviour faire being dissipate.

Only if half done wasn't that easy
If swotting wasn't thin on the ground
If trial wasn't a mess
Then might Candies weren't that sour..!!

-Shruti Soni

Misfortune!

When misfortune obstruck my way
Making my mind doomed
In that dark time , i will hang on
Till it twitches back and bloom.

- Shruti Soni

In the dark!

In the world full of stars
High in the sky
She was one of them
Twinkling like the other
Yet different.
Coruscating colours of life
Obscured with precariousness of the other moment
Yet she is still but addled
Savouring the stars of her life
Abruptly she quit !
Quit the whole sky
In middle of a song
In middle of a novel
Or in middle of a story !
She left ; like an incomplete glory !
U never know , when is your last day , last good day or
another decent day !

- Shruti Soni

A drop pure red still impure....

A throbbing day
being traumatic
carrying along untold happening

For you feel shy
wordless and mum
For the world
chiding you for the
bounty of almighty

Your sugary hold
instantly being root of
Impurete` and depravity

A drop pure red still impure
But for you gold holds no allure

For the temples and churches
filled with her wishes
It's the time
Go and bestow her a note
confessing
For the society may believe it an ordeal
But for me its the root i am flourishing
and your soul purely clear

Clarified and Real.

A drop pure red
Admire and Adore...!!
                                    32

       -Shruti Soni

Your efficacious soul.

Those unwelcomed emotions
Playing on you
Holding you to not to run
Neverthless
Your efficacious soul
Will fight and fight
Not ready to capitulate
Untill you make it right!

- Shruti Soni

Moon's Amity!

Calm and tranquil night
Carrying Moon on its midway
With stars as catalyst
I got an untold mate
To listen my prattle
Careless of my fate.
I went on gossiping
Adoring the placidity
Being drowsy
Natheless
I enjoyed the amity
Slowly pretermiting the time spot
I went on dozzing intermittently.

- Shruti Soni

Why not now

U said u love being silly !
U said u love being loved !
U said u want to dance !
And love to live !
Why not now ?
Holding back for a perfect chance ?
Swithering to cease another trance ?
Break the uncertainties
Silly yet fun
Pure at heart
This is the idyllic moment
Dance and turn
Be the one , ready to start !

- Shruti Soni

A Sweat ; Happy & Adore

Twinkling down from forehead
Slays away in air
A pure blend Of Diligent
Angelic & Natural
Her Sweat
Happy & Adore.

Her longings often veiled under smirk
With her duties endless
and trouble countless
Carrying along buckets
filled with untold patches of time
Yet her soul
Unstoppable.
Unraveling Gordian knot
Her Sweat
Happy & Adore.

Espousing at times of succour
Unbreakable she
Compromising with raptures
Yet her Sweat
Happy & Adore.

Manifest of epitome of love & protection

Resignation bound with death
Reminisce the icon
When near to last breathe.

Riddles caged in a bottle
far in sea fasten & strayed
Wisdom and wit touches her feet
for her Sweat
Wet & Pure
Happy & Adore.

His infancy
mixed with her Sweat
Reminiscing his memories
He turned 17
She believing it was his birthday
But for him
He celebrated his Mother's Day..!!

*Mother's day is not a defined day ...it's the day she becomes a mother ..!!

-Shruti Soni

.

Golden days..!

Repose near the sea
Negligent of all the happenings
Off track from the current situation
Watching the bees

Musing about the old days
Quite and calm
Full of games
With a mind
Free of all pains

Taking a trip down the memory lane
Recollecting all the shines
The time that spends
With the quiet old friends

Glued in midst of a hefty thought
The fallacy among friends
That became the reason they fought

Those were the days
Without any haze
But today the long down walk
is full of maze

Days were golden not
Because they had a shine
But spent with those
Precious "idiots" of mine

-Shruti Soni

Soul is immortal, But shell is not.

The way clouds travel
Different routes different places
Inevitable
Separating and again maneuvering
Similarly
The soul is immortal
But the shell is not
With that endless journey
It travels carrying along empty buckets
Filled and refilled
For this is the rule
Followed by all
Focused by none
End no. Of relations
Breaking away
Or forming a new one
Trying to reminisce
But one cannot
The soul is immortal
But the shell is not.

Think , try , understand. The rule of universe .
Many ages passed away we being alive but with memories
of present , brainwash about past . Life is short but the
journey is vast , the soul is not but the shell is new, known

by few.
(Teachings of Krishna - Bhagavad Gita)

Shruti Soni

Survive and strive!

The feeling of being exhausted
Wrapping all over you
Tired and chaotic
Fighting and surviving
Brawling with your inner voice, get up
and start striving for a better you.

-Shruti Soni

Someone..!

Darker the nights
Beautiful are the mornings
For mesmerizing evenings
You need someone's twinning !

-Shruti Soni

Mentor!

I doubted my own self
Lost on unworldly paths
But then
Their trust were the candle
Igniting my hopes
With all their efforts
Clearing my sight
I was able to achieve all my heights.

-Shruti Soni

The unspoken scars..!

After many struggles she was out carrying along her unscreamed story she was weighed down by the society ..
Being a girl was her destiny
But the society caught her in tyranny and her scars speaks...

For my body was a toy
Which they enjoy
I wear shorts
they turn me into a corpse.
The defination of mine
is changed with time
For they called it novelty
I find it cruelty
The only fault of my
Was to fly high.
For i shout , i cry , i rush , i try
to see the sky
For my soul was in a state of delicacy
But they don't have a spark of decency
as claiming my end
was now their trend...!

- Shruti Soni

Unstoppable!

It was calm clear and tranquil
The ocean , waves , birds , sand and her
Conceptualizing and unfolding her dream
With experiences of worst and full of thirst
A soul was build
Full of concrete
Ready to beat.

- Shruti Soni

Caged Wings.

Beneath that limitless sky
Clouds blocking the rays
Wondering down the lane
Her money and fame .

Conquering heights gave her happiness
Yet she was caged with wings
Making house her limit
They teach her to be
quiet weak and light.

Being a girl was her destiny
But the society caught her in tyranny
Having Ocean deep dreams
Yet fussed with small minds
She got her wings
Captured and bind.

Carrying along untold patches of time
She was shattered into pieces
Natheless
Unstoppable
She reached there
With limpid thoughts
She realised

Chain the wings
To be the master of rings.

- Shruti Soni

Reunion of US!

I saw her
The same her
Withholding our feelings
Our eyes whispered most of it.

It all started with the primary phase
Her first glance captivated me
It was like a sweet music
Soothing my soul
Yet unable to recognise.

Years passed
We tied in a knot of friendship
Happy but somewhere incomplete
Incomplete the way
Moon is without its shine
Nature is without its beauty.

Biding farewell to each other
We walked contrary
Concealing our emotions
longing for the old days.

I saw the same her
Time was unable to steal the shine

It was a reunion
Reunion of concealed feelings
Reunion of us.

Numbers exchanged
Once again
She stole my heart
But this time
It was not only me;
The time confirmed it.

Finally we reunited
But in a different aspect
Eventually entering in a new phase
Starting with primary
It lasted till eternity.

- Shruti Soni

Greed!

Planting a seed
In greed of that fruit
But somewhere in the ground
That tiny pixels of fertilizers and chemicals
Corrupting the roots
giving rise to sour fruit.

-Shruti Soni

Failure.

Try to taste failure once
For the sun too sets
After its triumph...

Its not everytime you need to worry
Take a deep breathe and rest for a while..!!

-Shruti Soni

Typhoon!

The typhoon of your soul
And the waves at the shore
Performing their chores
Relaxing and looking at the shoal
Carrying it whole.

- Shruti Soni

Far flung Friends!

Bags packed , pony high , button up shirt !!

A pure blend of diligent
Drops pure white
Clear and bright
Full of happiness yet sad
Moments to reminisce
Our friendship is our pride .
Memories full of laughter
In blink of an eye
Clock twisted and time was faster
Yet
No matter where , no matter how
Shine to my smiles
Together for miles.

-Shruti Soni

Long way down!

Got a long way down
Deep inside my brain
Puzzled between thoughts
What is wrong what is right.

Sitting beneath the blue sky
Glued in midst of brain and heart
Misplaced among varied verdicts of life.

Right away the adjoining minute
Something became the cause of my smirk
The blow of freezing breeze
The song of tranquil nature
Instantaneously solving the puzzle
Maneuvering my thoughts
Solving my cause.

Yet got a long way down
Deep inside my brain
To be covered by me again.

- Shruti Soni

Reminiscing Hour.

Bygone in thoughts
Admiring the beauty
The rhapsodies of the moment
Making you ecstatic
Suddenly gloomy and dejected
For you lost it to your fate.

- Shruti Soni

The Moulding Hammer.

On that hapeless night
A sense of fragility
Serendipitous
His fingers entangled
Fostering a chivalrous shell
He gave me strength
Breaking the chain
With his impetus couch
He washed away all my strain.

- Shruti Soni

Memories!

Sometimes
Enduring memories reminisce
lost in woods , isolated
far unworldly
Leaving behind us
dumbstruck and dismay !!

- Shruti Soni

Heaven's Water!

Drops touching my finger
with that soothing sound
roads wet
somewhere in the corner
water moulding in its own way....

That heart touching petrichor
Drops twinkling down
Tickling my lips
and my eyes
Capturing that mesmerizing Rainbow..!!

The wet road with little smell of sand
Leading towards peace in your heart
Chasing the winds with flowers
The air touches your hair with a sweet song
Carrying towards mental peace !!

- Shruti Soni

Hold on!

Take a break
And hold one breathe
Feel the moment
Cause they are your real wreath !

Moment of cry
And the other of joy
Don't hold them
Cause they are always meant to fly !

As when soul breaks down
It can be a chance to rebuild
In a better way.

-Shruti Soni

Its OKAY!

Its okay to cry through your flaws
Or to regret all your wars,
Its okay to feel shy sometimes
And take a rest from all your wines.
Its okay to scuffle with your kink with an intention to win!

- Shruti Soni